To Joel,
Let your heartbeat
guide your feet!
Love, Tammy
xoxo

By Tammy Laframboise
Illustrations by Steve Bermundo
Book Design by Jayme LaForest

Raspberry
Books

Raspberry
Books

Text and illustrations Copyright ©2013 by Tammy Laframboise.
All rights reserved. No part of this publication may be reproduced, stored in a retrieval system, or transmitted, in any form or by any means whatsoever without prior written permission from the publisher.
Published in the United States by Raspberry Books.
ISBN-13: 978-0-9848749-1-0

Manufactured in the United States of America

We sleep with his voice dancing in our heads
and wake to our feet tapping in our beds.
To Mr. Al Gilbert, the Pied Piper of Dance,
and my friend.
–T.L.

I would like to dedicate these illustrations
to all the tap dancers in the world
who give their feet a voice
–S.B.

Hi, my name is Popsy
And oooOO I really can't wait
Today is my first Tap class
I just know it's gonna be great!

These shoes are super cool
Cause I get to make lots of noise
Like CLICK, pop, ziggy do BOP
And...

I go to class to learn my steps
And listen really close
To the sounds I make with
Heel Push Walks
and Backward Knocking Toes

I push the petal to the metal
And take off around the room.

Backward Knocking Toes are a cinch
Just knock them left to right
Snap your fingers for some pep
And you'll look outta sight

Sometimes you get a tricky step
Like the dreaded and treacherous Flap

Good thing I met a friend to help
And he says "Tap Is A Snap!"

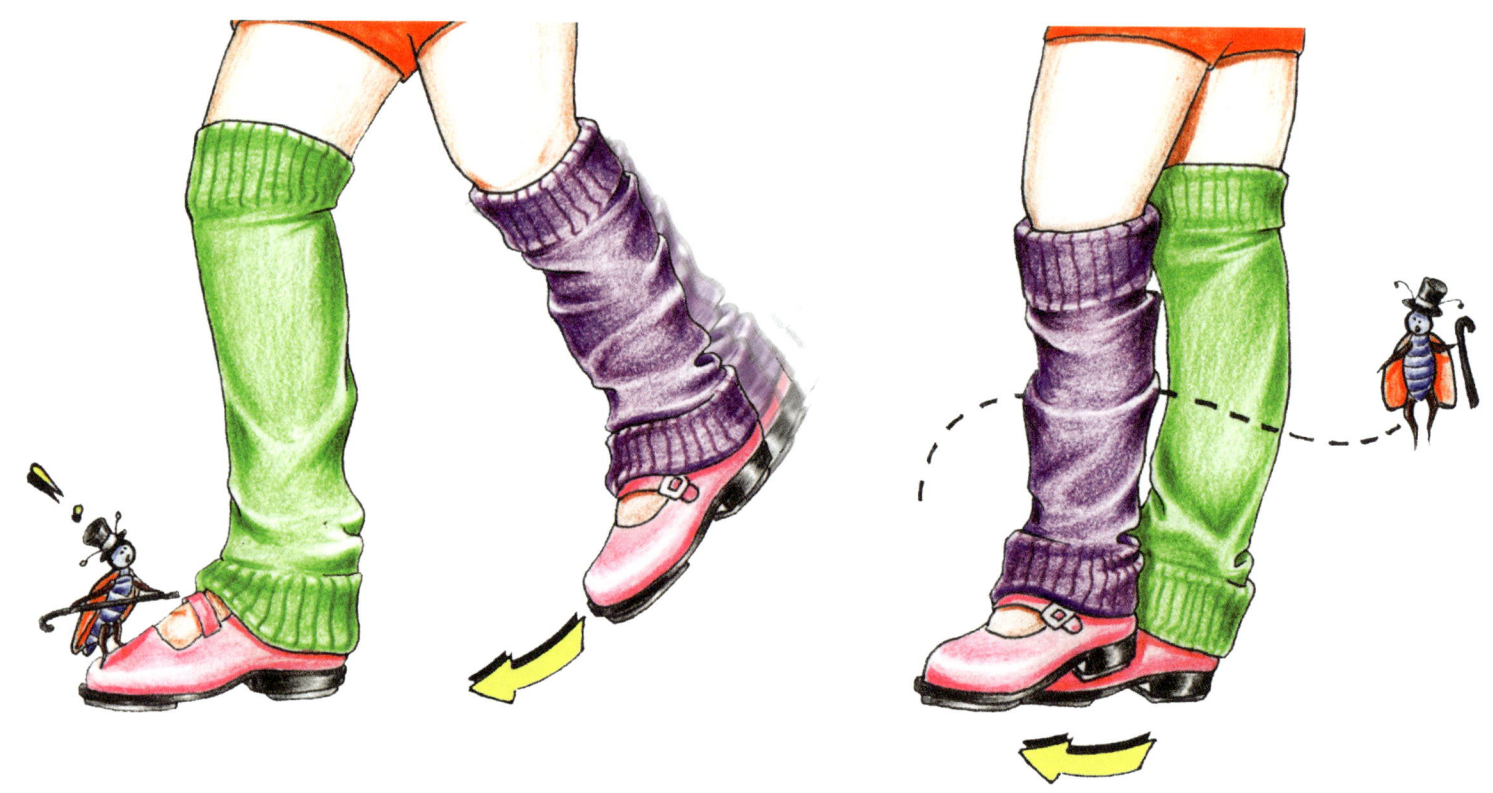

To Flap you brush your toes

Then **SLAP** they go on the floor

Be careful not to squish that bug

Or he won't get to dance anymore

My new friend showed me lots of things
His name is Benny D
Like dropping one heel at a time
Is how you Boogie Woogie

He taught me how to Gallop
And sound like a trotting horse
One foot chases the other
And say 'giddy up' of course

Benny D is VERY good
At doing Side Heel Digs
He taps his heels from side to side
Like a pro who's made it big

We've really been working hard
So we take a deep breath
To Ballchange

Rock back and front
Just like Gene Kelly
And you're singin' in the rain

Now let's learn Cramp Roll
Up up down down is fun to do
Like our feet are on a rollercoaster

That was super fun
But no more clownin' around

This next one needs our focus
Just so we don't fall down

Pick up one foot to Shuffle
While the mice run up the clock
Brush front and back a bunch to hear...

Now we're ready for Irish
So we do a Shuffle to start
Then, like the Lord of the Dance, Hop Step
And let the drum beat fill your heart

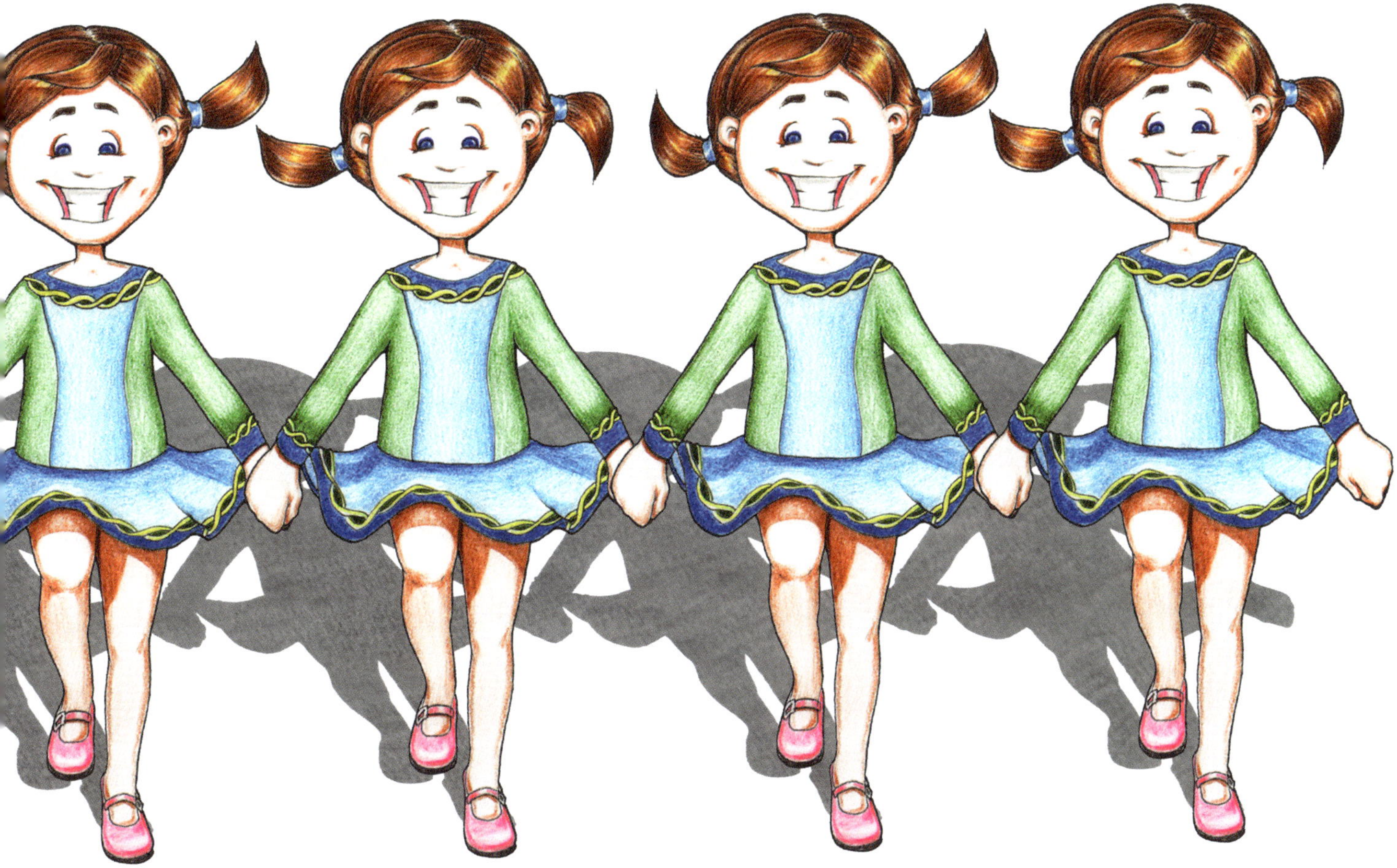

It's Maxi Ford time now
So I better ask Benny D

He Says Maxi Ford is
"Just as easy as can be"

Tick, Tock, Switch, Knock
And you're more than half way there
Now top it off with Step and Clap
To show a little **FLAIR**

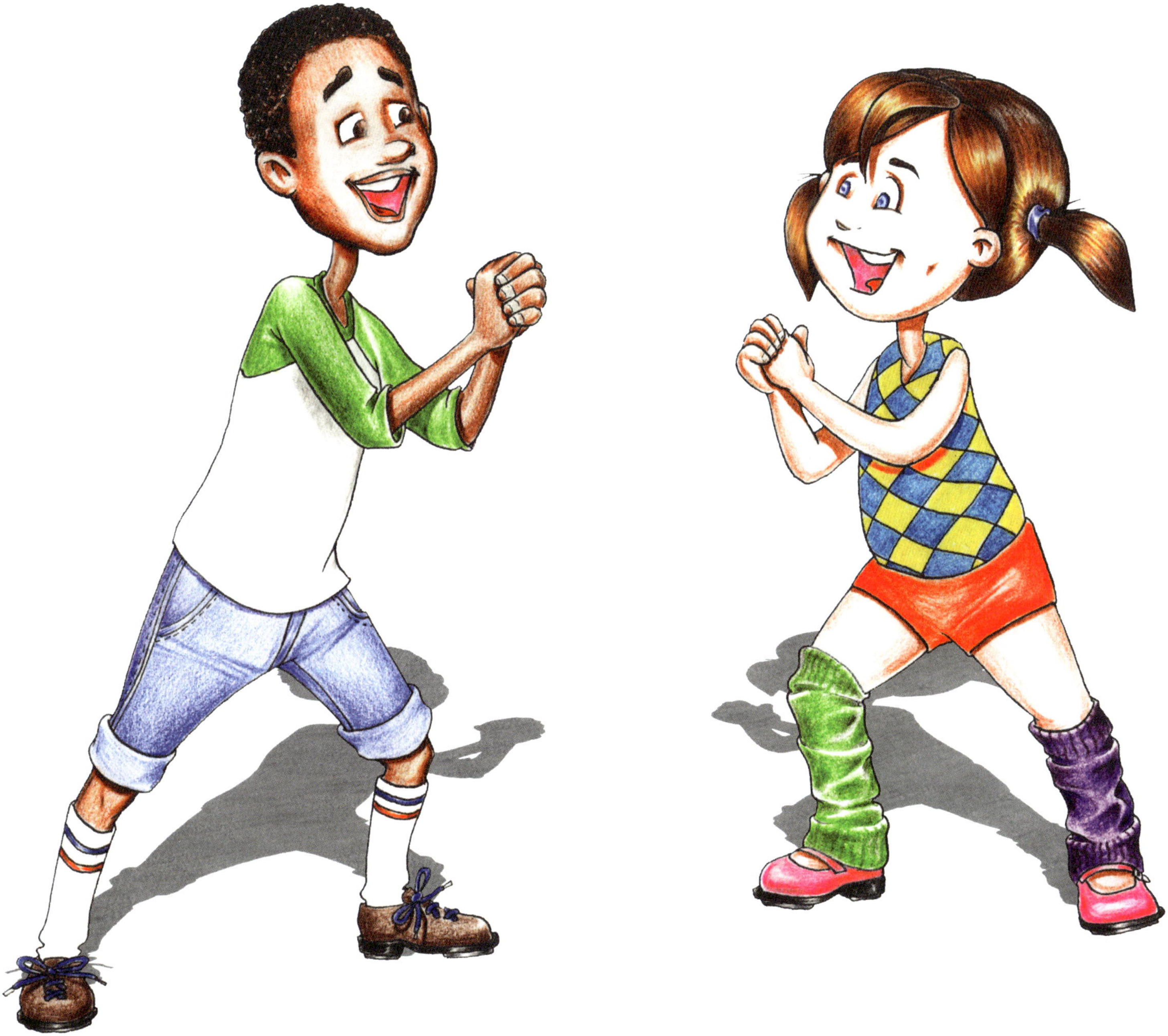

And now for the big show-stopper
That good ol' Flash Trick Step

Down, back, scoot, jump up
And they'll treat you like a CELEB!

Now that we know lots of steps
We can make a routine
We'll do our Shuffle Ballchange step
And the crowd will clap and scream

"Shuffle"

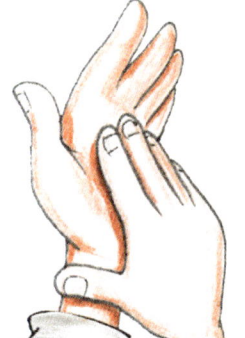

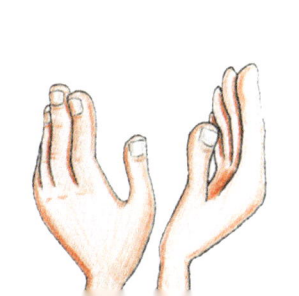

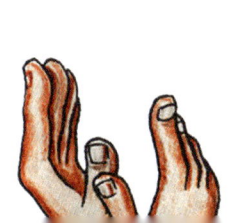

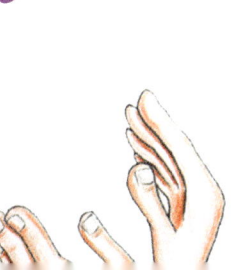

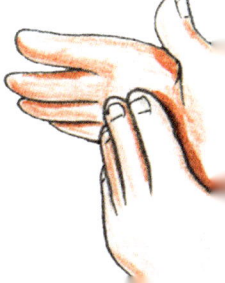

"Ballchange"

We'll show our Side Heel Digs and Gallops
Cramp Rolls, Knock Backs and Flaps

"Flap"

"Gallop"

"Side Heel Digs"

"Cramp Roll"

We'll Maxi Ford, Irish and Heel Push Walk
Until we wear out our taps

"Irish"

"Maxi Ford"

"Backward Knocking Toes"

"Heel Push Walks"

"Flash Trick Step"

Don't forget that Flash Trick Step
Or the Boogie Woogie

"Boogie Woogie"

And now the audience is on their feet
With a...

WHOOP!

WHOOP!!

WHOOPIE!!!

So it's time to close the show
But oh, there's one more thing

Feet together and take a Bow
Cause you were A-MA-ZING!

THANK YOU to my family and friends for their constant support. And to Steve Bermundo for continuing on this journey with me. A special thank you to my sounding boards Jayme LaForest and Lori Yearwood. Thank you also to someone who is not only a character in real life, but has allowed me to turn him into a fictional one too, Benny Doherty. I love and appreciate each of you.

TAMMY LAFRAMBOISE was born in Windsor, Ontario, Canada. She began dancing at the age of 11 and immediately fell in love with it! She began teaching dance at the age of 18 and also began a professional dance career around the same time. After graduating college Tammy moved to Los Angeles, California to further pursue her dance career. She is currently living, dancing and teaching dance in L.A. For more of Popsy please visit www.popsybooks.com

STEVE BERMUNDO is a self taught illustrator. He's spent most of his adult life as a professional dancer, having performed all around the world, eventually returning to his first love... drawing. He has already lent his illustrating talents to several authors. You can see more of his work at www.BearMoonDoe.com

Made in the USA
San Bernardino, CA
11 July 2014